Ralph Braun

easterseals

CHERRY LAKE PRESS

Published in the United States of America by Cherry Lake Publishing Group
Ann Arbor, Michigan
www.cherrylakepublishing.com

Reading Adviser: Beth Walker Gambro, MS, Ed., Reading Consultant, Yorkville, IL
Book Designer: Jennifer Wahi
Illustrator: Jeff Bane

Photo Credits: © Roberto Galan/Shutterstock, 5; © Dan76/Shutterstock, 7; © Evgeny Atamanenko/Shutterstock, 9; National Museum of American History, Smithsonian Institution, 11, 13, 21, 22; © oliverdelahaye/Shutterstock, 15; © Christopher Halloran/Shutterstock, 17; © Jose Gil/Shutterstock, 19, 23

Cherry Lake Press is an imprint of Cherry Lake Publishing Group.

Library of Congress Cataloging-in-Publication Data

Names: Trockman, Ben, author. | Bane, Jeff, 1957- illustrator.
Title: Ralph Braun / by Ben Trockman ; illustrated by Jeff Bane.
Description: Ann Arbor, Michigan : Cherry Lake Publishing, [2023] | Series: My itty-bitty bio | Audience: Grades K-1 | Summary: "Ralph Braun, an inventor and businessman, revolutionized mobility for disabled people. This biography for early readers examines his life in a simple, age-appropriate way that helps young readers develop word recognition and reading skills. Developed in partnership with Easterseals and written by a member of the disability community, this title helps all readers learn from those who make a difference in our world. The My Itty-Bitty Bio series celebrates diversity, inclusion, and the values that readers of all ages can aspire to"-- Provided by publisher.
Identifiers: LCCN 2023009123 | ISBN 9781668927311 (hardcover) | ISBN 9781668928363 (paperback) | ISBN 9781668929834 (ebook) | ISBN 9781668931318 (pdf)
Subjects: LCSH: Braun, Ralph W. | Inventors--United States--Biography--Juvenile literature. | Motor scooters--Juvenile literature. | People with disabilities--United States--Biography--Juvenile literature. | Muscular dystrophy--Patients--United States--Biography--Juvenile literature.
Classification: LCC T40.B65 T76 2023 | DDC 609.2--dc23/eng/20230413
LC record available at https://lccn.loc.gov/2023009123

Printed in the United States of America
Corporate Graphics

table of contents

About the author: When he's not writing, making jokes, or public speaking, Ben Trockman works in the communications industry. Ben also serves as a city councilman in his hometown of Evansville, Indiana.

About the illustrator: Jeff Bane and his two business partners own a studio along the American River in Folsom, California, home of the 1849 Gold Rush. When Jeff's not sketching or illustrating for clients, he's either swimming or kayaking in the river to relax.

About our partnership: This title was developed in partnership with Easterseals to support its mission of empowering people with disabilities. Through their national network of affiliates, Easterseals provides essential services and on-the-ground supports to more than 1.5 million people each year.

I was born in Winamac, Indiana. My family farmed. At age 6, I walked slow. Stairs were hard for me.

I had **muscular dystrophy**. It is a **disability**. It made my muscles weak.

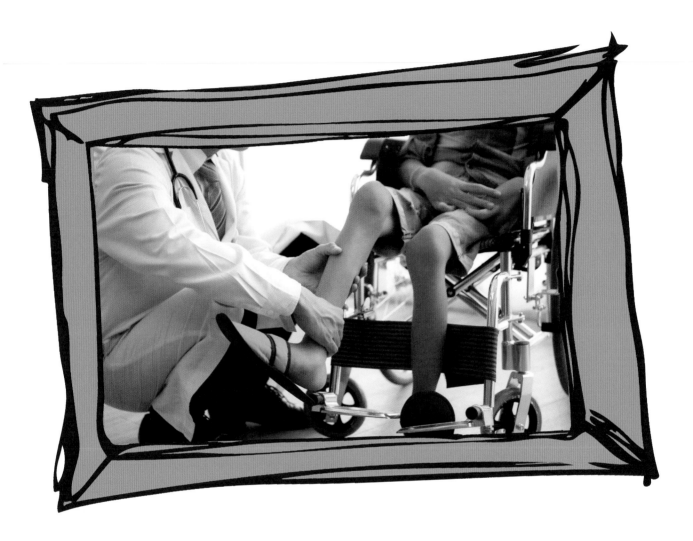

My parents didn't give up. They didn't let me give up. My parents were my **heroes**.

Who is your hero?

My mom had seven brothers. They fixed cars. I learned to fix things. I **invented** an electric scooter.

What would you like to invent?

I helped make a special van.
It lifted wheelchair users. Then,
I invented a way I could drive.

I started a company. It still makes vans. It is called BraunAbility.

What would you name
your business?

I loved racing. My son and I owned a NASCAR team. We called it Braun Racing.

In 2012, I got an award. President Barack Obama named me a "**Champion** of Change."

I died in 2013. My **legacy** lives on. I didn't give up. I inspire others to never give up!

What would you like to ask me?

1963

1940

Born
1940

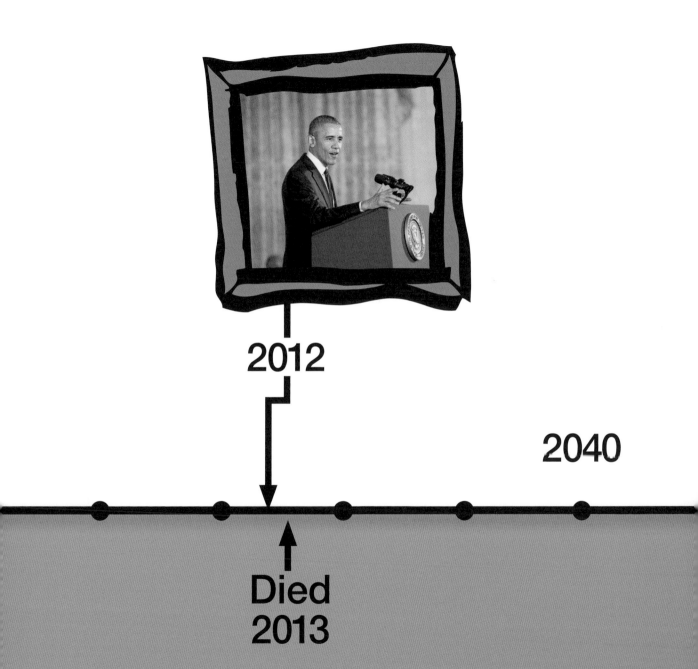

2012

2040

Died
2013

glossary

champion (CHAMP-ee-uhn) someone who fights for another

disability (dis-uh-BIL-uh-tee) a condition that limits a person's movements, senses, or activities

heroes (HEAR-ohs) people someone admire and want to be like

invented (in-VENT-ed) created something new

legacy (LE-guh-see) something passed down from one generation to the next

muscular dystrophy (MUS-kyoo-ler DIS-troh-fee) a condition where muscles get weaker and weaker over time

index